Special Dedication

This book is dedicated to my wife and daughter whose love I cannot live without.

One sunny day, a boy named Jack decided to go on a journey with his little dog, Spot. They wanted to explore the world and meet all sorts of animals and people. They knew that every encounter would be an adventure and might even teach them something new.

First, they met Mr. Oliver, the old owl, who lived on the tallest branch of a mighty oak tree. Mr. Oliver had wise, round eyes that seemed to see everything. He taught Jack and Spot about patience. "Sometimes," said Mr. Oliver, "the best things come to those who wait."

Next, they met Sally, the sly squirrel. Sally was always bustling around, collecting acorns and hopping from branch to branch. From her, Jack and Spot learned the value of hard work and preparation. "It's important to save for a rainy day," she said, wagging her fluffy tail.

As Jack and Spot continued their journey, they came across a pond where they met Delia, the dazzling dancing duck. Delia would sway and twirl on the water, leaving ripples behind. From Delia, they learned the joy of expressing oneself. "Always be true to who you are," she quacked with a smile.

By the pond, they also encountered Frank, the friendly frog. Frank had a deep voice and loved singing in the evenings. He taught them about harmony and finding one's unique voice. "You don't need to be the loudest," croaked Frank, "just be the truest."

Further down the road, they met the Baker family. Mrs. Baker baked the most delicious pies and Mr. Baker played delightful tunes on his guitar. Their children, Lily and Lucas, played and laughed, spreading joy. The Bakers shared their pie and stories with Jack and Spot, teaching them the value of sharing and community. "When you share, you multiply happiness," said Mrs. Baker, offering them another slice of pie.

On the edge of the forest, they encountered Gary, the giant but gentle gorilla. Gary looked tough with his huge arms and broad chest, but he had a soft heart. He taught Jack and Spot not to judge by appearances. "It's what's inside that counts," he said, giving them a tender hug.

As they crossed a meadow, they met Bella, the beautiful butterfly. Bella had once been a caterpillar and told them her story of transformation. She taught them about change and the beauty of new beginnings. "Every ending," she fluttered, "is also a new start."

The sun was beginning to set, and Jack and Spot decided to head home. On their way, they encountered Old Mrs. Wilson, the elderly lady from their neighborhood. She had kind, crinkly eyes and always carried sweets in her pockets. As they sat with her on her porch, she spoke of the past and all the lessons she had learned over the years. "Remember, dear ones," she said, "every person and every creature you meet has a story and a lesson to offer. Always listen with an open heart."

Jack and Spot reached home with their hearts full of gratitude. They had learned so much from all the wonderful animals and people they had met. As they snuggled in their beds, they promised each other to always be curious, kind, and open to the lessons that life offered.

And so, every day became an adventure, and every encounter a new lesson, for Jack and his little dog, Spot.

THE END